MW00989080

# TRUE TEEN STORIES

# TRUE STORIES OF
# Teen Prisoners

John Micklos Jr.

Cavendish
Square
New York

Published in 2018 by Cavendish Square Publishing, LLC
243 5th Avenue, Suite 136, New York, NY 10016

Copyright © 2018 by Cavendish Square Publishing, LLC

First Edition

Website: cavendishsq.com

This publication represents the opinions and views of the author based on his or her personal
experience, knowledge, and research. The information in this book serves as a general
guide only. The author and publisher have used their best efforts in preparing this book and
disclaim liability rising directly or indirectly from the use and application of this book.

All websites were available and accurate when this book was sent to press.

Cataloging-in-Publication Data

Names: Micklos Jr, John.
Title: True stories of teen prisoners / John Micklos Jr.
Description: New York : Cavendish Square, 2018. | Series: True teen stories | Includes index.
Identifiers: ISBN 9781502631602 (library bound)
| ISBN 9781502634030 (pbk.) | ISBN 9781502631619 (ebook)
Subjects: LCSH: Juvenile delinquency--United States--Juvenile literature. | Juvenile
delinquents--United States--Juvenile literature. | Juvenile justice, Administration of--United
States--Juvenile literature. | Juvenile corrections--United States--Juvenile literature.
Classification: LCC HV9104.M53 2018 | DDC 364.360973--dc23

Editorial Director: David McNamara
Editor: Caitlyn Miller
Copy Editor: Alex Tessman
Associate Art Director: Amy Greenan
Designer: Deanna Paternostro
Production Coordinator: Karol Szymczuk
Photo Research: J8 Media

The photographs in this book are used by permission and through the courtesy of: Cover Shepard
Sherbell/CORBIS SABA/Getty Images; p. 4 Felipe Caparrós/AGE Fotostock; p. 8 Daytona Beach
News-Journal, Jessica Webb Sibley/AP Images; p. 13 Hulton Archive/Getty Images; p. 18 LM Otero/
AP Images; p. 20 Darren Greenwood/Getty Images; p. 23 Laurence Kesterson/MCT/Newscom; p.
24 Wavebreakmedia/Shutterstock.com; p. 28 Fototeca Gilardi/Getty Images; p. 30 Grandriver/Getty
Images; p. 33 Jose Luis Magana/AP Images; p. 36 Gary Doak/Alamy Stock Photo; p. 40 Sharon
Steinmann/ZUMAPRESS.com; p. 45 Paul Kern/Alamy Stock Photo; p. 46 Rich Legg/Getty Images;
p. 49 The Jefferson City News-Tribune, Julie Smith/AP Images; p. 57 Marmaduke St. John/Alamy
Stock Photo; p. 58 Jiawangkun/Shutterstock.com; p. 61 Mlenny/Getty Images; p. 62 Olivier Asselin/
Alamy Stock Photo; p. 67 Jeff Holt/Bloomberg/Getty Images; p. 71 José Nicolas/Sygma/Getty
Images; p. 73 A.M. Ahad/AP Images; p. 76 Shehzad Noorani/Majority World/UIG/Getty Images; p. 84
Scott Olson/Getty Images; p. 85 Cecil Bo Dzwowa/Shutterstock.com; p. 90 Helen H. Richardson/The
Denver Post/Getty Images; p. 93 Rawpixel.com/Shutterstock.com; p. 95 Miqu77/Shutterstock.com.

Printed in the United States of America

# CONTENTS

# Freedom, Choice, and Privacy

When most teens awake in the morning, a world of opportunity awaits. It might not seem that way at first; with school and activities, the day may seem highly structured. In reality, most teens have a day filled with choices, choosing what to eat for breakfast and lunch. At school, teens probably have some choice in the classes they take. In the afternoon, they may participate in sports or some other afterschool activity they have chosen. Then come dinner, homework, and probably some free time to watch television, play video games, or relax. The vast majority of teenagers can decide what to watch or do with that leisure time. If they want privacy, they simply go into their bedroom and close the door. Overall, most teens have a high degree of choice, freedom, and privacy.

Teens in prison or juvenile detention centers face a far different reality. They have no freedom to choose where they go or what they do. Their days really are highly structured. From the moment they

*Opposite*: Teen prisoners lose their physical freedom, their choice, and their privacy while incarcerated.

get up until the time until they go to bed, each hour of their day is scheduled, and even if they have "free time," they have limited choices for how to spend it. Incarcerated teens also have almost no privacy: other inmates surround them. Surveillance cameras track their movements. In fact, they rarely have a moment when they aren't being monitored.

Freedom, choice, and privacy. Those are the biggest differences between life inside a detention center or prison and life outside. Of course, choice is why most youth find themselves imprisoned in the first place. They made bad choices and engaged in illegal activities. One goal of incarceration is to give their lives structure—lots of structure. The intention is that when teen prisoners are released, they will maintain the discipline to make better choices on the outside.

Teens get placed in detention centers for a variety of reasons. One might be there for shoplifting, while another might have committed armed robbery. One might have gotten into fights in school, and another might be a member of a gang. Some abused alcohol or drugs; others sold drugs. Some teens may be there for actions that aren't "true" crimes, such as running away.

Teen offenders come in all shapes and sizes. As a group, however, they tend to have several things in common. First of all, most are male. The number of male teens in prisons and juvenile detention centers in the United States outnumbers females by more than two to one. Second, many incarcerated teens are minorities. African American and American Indian youth are four times more likely than whites to be committed to secure placement facilities. Hispanic youth are 61 percent more likely to be imprisoned than white youth.

Many incarcerated teens come from broken homes. Some have been abused, either physically, sexually, or emotionally. Some have grown up in foster care, and these teens might have bounced from place to place without ever having a home or family they could truly call their own. Other teens have run away from home seeking a better life.

Many troubled teens struggle in school. They often lack effective reading skills. The further they progress in school, they further behind they fall. Frustrated, they begin skipping school—or drop out altogether. Often, dropouts get caught up in gangs, drugs, or other illegal activities.

Addressing the problem of teen incarceration is complicated and can seem overwhelming. Many experts argue that by the time youth are in prison it's already too late to truly help them. By that time, they have established bad habits that are hard to break. These experts suggest focusing on prevention rather than rehabilitation: offering universal preschool programs helps ensure that all youth enter school ready to learn. Offering family support services might mean that fewer youth come from broken homes. Providing health and nutrition programs for young children may improve their health and ensure they can reach their full potential. The catch is that comprehensive programs cost money. Advocates of such programs believe that the cost is worth it. They argue that investing money in the early stages of a child's life saves far more money later on.

The decisions that officials make in regard to teen crime prevention affect the lives of many people. More than half a million juveniles under the age of eighteen are arrested each year in the United States alone. There is no simple or single solution to the problem of incarcerated teens. The scope of the issue, however, demands that we continue to search for answers.

# CHAPTER ONE

# Teens in Prison Today

J uvenile crime in the United States presents a "good news, bad news" situation. The good news is that the crime rate for juveniles has dropped dramatically over the past twenty years. Violent crimes among juveniles peaked in the early and mid-1990s. Since then, the rate of violent juvenile crimes has dropped by more than 50 percent, according to statistics from the government's Office of Juvenile Justice and Delinquency Prevention (OJJDP). Violent crimes include murder, manslaughter, rape, robbery, and aggravated assault.

The bad news is that juvenile crime remains a significant problem. FBI crime statistics indicate that nearly 650,000 people under the age of eighteen were arrested in 2015. Meanwhile, more than 54,000 juveniles served time in

*Opposite*: More than half a million teens are arrested each year in the United States alone, making juvenile justice a vital issue.

juvenile detention centers or prisons in 2013, according to OJJDP data.

It also helps to consider juvenile crime in the context of adult crime. The United States has the world's highest rate of overall incarceration. In 2013, the United States jailed 716 people per 100,000. The worldwide average is around 160. About 4.4 percent of the world's population lives in the United States; however, the nation houses more than one out of every five of the world's prisoners. As of 2016, nearly 2.3 million people were incarcerated in the United States, according to the Prison Policy Initiative.

World Prison Brief data shows that other countries with high incarceration rates include El Salvador (574 people per 100,000), Cuba (510), and the Russian Federation (433). The incarceration rates of major US allies are far lower. England's incarceration rate stands at 146 people per 100,000, Canada's is 114, Italy's is 92, Germany's rate is 76, and Japan's is 45. Many politicians and sociologists find these statistics alarming. In 2013, former Virginia Senator Jim Webb said, "We are either the most evil people in the world or there is something fundamentally wrong with our criminal justice system."

Of course, these numbers represent adult criminals. The figures for juvenile offenders are much harder to obtain and compare. Different countries compute them differently. Still, it's safe to say that the United States also has a relatively high rate of juvenile incarceration compared to other countries. It's also safe to assume that many of the adult criminals in the United States began their life of crime as juveniles.

# JUVENILE JUSTICE THROUGHOUT HISTORY

As long as there have been people on Earth, there has been crime. Some of that crime has always been committed by juveniles. The concept of a separate justice system for juveniles, however, is actually fairly new. For centuries, parents treated children like little adults and authorities did the same. If children broke a law, they received the same punishment as adults. In England in the 1600s, young people who stole things could be whipped or put in stocks in the town square. For some offenses, they could be put in prison. Children who committed violent crimes could be punished by death, just as adults were.

That same concept carried over to colonial America. Treatment of juvenile criminals varied from colony to colony. New England colonies tended to have strict rules about how people should behave, and those rules extended to children. In seventeenth-century Massachusetts, a child could be sentenced to death simply for cursing at his or her parents. Children who stole or committed other offenses could find themselves in prison alongside adults.

The policy of treating juvenile offenders the same as adults continued into the nineteenth century. In fact, one researcher estimated that more than 100 children were executed for crimes during this time span. Most of those who were executed had committed murder. Yet to many people, such harsh punishments seemed out of place for children, regardless of their crime. By the 1800s, social reformers began focusing on improving the lives of children. They wanted to prevent children from working long hours in mills or mines, and they fought to ensure that all children had an opportunity to attend school. Reformers wanted young people who committed crimes to be treated differently than adults: instead of placing juvenile offenders with adult criminals, activists wanted to create special facilities to house juveniles who broke the law.

In 1825, New York City established the New York House of Refuge. This institution housed poor youth who authorities thought might be headed toward delinquency, and soon other major cities followed suit. These institutions became known as **reform schools**. The idea was to help at-risk youth reform their behavior before they got into serious trouble. In theory, this makes sense. Removing young people from unstable or abusive home environments allows them to live in safety, giving them an opportunity to turn their lives around. Over time, however, many of these facilities became overcrowded. In others, juveniles faced abuse. In some cases, they were no safer in the reform school than they were outside. Because of these concerns, states gradually began taking over the responsibility for these facilities; ultimately, many reform schools were shut down.

Meanwhile, the way courts handled cases changed as well. Until the late nineteenth century, the same criminal courts tried both youth and adults. Social reformers fought for a separate court system for juveniles in the hope that such a system could be more sensitive to the specialized needs of young people.

Many reformers saw juvenile delinquents as a product of their environment. Delinquency, they believed, stemmed from factors such as poverty, lack of education, and unstable home environments. These reformers hoped that a justice system designed specifically to meet the needs of juveniles could provide help and rehabilitation. In some cases, they still recommended placing delinquents in reformatories, a solution that they did

Young boys used to be incarcerated in adult prisons, as seen in this illustration of London's Tothill Fields Prison from 1845.

not view as punishment. Rather, they believed that this offered the best chance for the young people to have a better life.

## THE PENDULUM SWINGS

In 1899, the state of Illinois approved passage of the Juvenile Court Act. This act established the nation's first true juvenile justice system and set a model that other states followed over time. The goal of the juvenile justice system was to provide rehabilitation and protective supervision for young people. Almost all juvenile cases were handled by individual judges rather than by jury trials. Judges determined whether offenders would be placed in a detention facility or receive probation.

Since the mid-twentieth century, the pendulum has swung back and forth regarding how juvenile offenders should be treated. By the 1960s, concern had grown about leaving so much discretion in the hands of judges because sentences varied widely from judge to judge. Some judges seemed to give harsher sentences to black and Hispanic youth. Many people thought that having a single person make the decision seemed unfair.

Over time, more juvenile offenders received full trials. Several high-profile Supreme Court cases extended the same protections to juveniles that adults received in the criminal justice system. In 1974, Congress passed the Juvenile Justice and Delinquency Prevention Act (JJDPA). The new law sought to guard the rights of juvenile offenders and their families while also upholding community safety. The JJDPA established a nationwide juvenile planning and advisory system and provided federal funding for delinquency prevention programs in individual states. In addition, the law authorized establishment of the OJJDP.

One key component of the new law was the deinstitutionalization of status offenders. A status offense is one that hinges on a person's status (in this case, their age). For example, truancy or running away are not crimes for adults. They are illegal only for young people, and authorities did not want juveniles placed in detention facilities for offenses such as these. They also did not juveniles jailed for other offenses, such as violating curfew laws or possessing alcohol or drugs.

Another component of the new law involved working to remove juveniles from adult jails and ensuring that young offenders did not have any contact with adult inmates. The law also focused on reducing the disproportionate number of minorities who became involved with the juvenile justice system. However, the climate changed in the 1980s. As crime rates rose, the public called for harsher treatment of criminals. As a result, many states passed "get tough" laws, and fewer people received probation. Instead, many crimes carried mandatory sentences. The "get tough" policies extended to juvenile offenders as well, and more juvenile cases were transferred to adult courts. By the mid-1990s, the number of youths held in juvenile detention centers—and adult prisons—had peaked.

By the early twenty-first century, the pendulum had swung yet again. Crime rates trended downward. States once again began to focus on rehabilitation rather than incarceration. Several states, including California, Hawaii, and Massachusetts, made major reforms in their juvenile justice systems. For instance, in 2007, California passed legislation limiting the types of offenders who could be committed to detention. It also provided funding for counties to develop innovative programs for dealing with juvenile concerns on a more local level.

## COURT CASES

Over the years, several cases pertaining to juvenile justice have found their way to the Supreme Court. The *Kent v. United States* case in 1966 granted juveniles who face criminal cases the right to legal counsel, but this ruling covered only federal cases. The next year, *In re Gault* extended all the same rights that adults have to juveniles accused of a crime. These include the right to an attorney, the right to cross examine witnesses testifying against the accused, and the right to remain silent (the Fifth Amendment right); the ruling covered state cases.

Another case established that juvenile trials, even ones involving serious crimes, do not have to be jury trials. But states do have the option to use jury trials with juvenile cases, and some states choose to do so. In another case in 1984, the Supreme Court ruled that schools could search a student's belongings as long as there was "reasonable" suspicion that the student was carrying something illegal.

Some more recent Supreme Court cases have also affected juvenile justice. In the 2005 *Roper v. Simmons* case, the Court ruled it unconstitutional for a youth under the age of eighteen to receive a death penalty sentence. In 2010, the Supreme Court ruled against sentencing a juvenile to life imprisonment with no possibility of **parole** for any crime other than **homicide**. The Court ruled that such a sentence violated the Eighth Amendment by being "cruel and unusual punishment." It stated that young offenders should have a chance to obtain release if they later showed "demonstrated maturity and rehabilitation." The case of *Miller v. Alabama* in 2012 extended that ruling. The Court made it unconstitutional to ever sentence someone who was under eighteen when the crime was committed to mandatory life in prison without parole.

## IMPRISONED WITH ADULTS

The 1980s and 1990s brought a "get tough" attitude toward crime, and this attitude included juvenile crime. Authorities believed that the best way to protect society was to put criminals in jail for as long as possible. Many criminal offenses carry a range of sentences, ranging from probation to varying amounts of time in prison. During this time period, judges rarely gave probation; instead, they often imposed the longest possible prison sentences.

The "get tough" policies had mixed results. After peaking in the mid-1990s, the crime rate did begin to fall. In fact, it fell dramatically across categories and age ranges, including juvenile offenders. Certainly, placing hardened criminals behind bars for longer periods prevented them from committing further crimes. However, many experts believe that many other factors also contributed to the drop in crime.

On the negative side, prisons were soon filled to overflowing. Given the high cost of incarceration, tougher sentencing cost taxpayers billions of extra dollars. Juvenile offenders also suffered from the "get tough" policies. For one thing, increasing numbers of juvenile cases were transferred to adult courts. In 1994, more than 12,000 cases received such treatment. That number had dropped to 7,600 by 2009.

In theory, courts transfer only the most serious juvenile cases to adult court. In practice, however, only half of the cases transferred in 2009 involved serious crimes. The other half involved less serious offenses. Furthermore, the decision to transfer cases to adult court seems gender based. Males are far more likely than females to have their cases transferred.

One factor that influences the transfer of cases to adult court involves the seriousness of the crime. A murder or rape case is far more likely to be transferred than a burglary or vandalism case. Another factor involves age: the older the juvenile offender, the more likely it is that the case will be transferred. This makes sense, since the juvenile would soon "age out" of the juvenile system anyway.

High-profile cases also are more likely to be transferred to the adult system. For instance, in 2013 teenager Ethan Couch was involved in a drunk driving crash that killed four people.

Ethan Couch, a teen involved in a drunk driving crash that killed four people, was tried as an adult after he turned nineteen.

At the time, Couch's lawyers used the defense that Couch had "affluenza." They said that he was so rich and spoiled that he didn't fully understand what he had done. Couch received a sentence of ten years of probation rather than a prison sentence.

In 2016, his case was moved to adult court when he turned nineteen. After he violated his probation, he received a jail sentence of nearly two years. His lawyers asked the Texas Supreme Court to overturn that decision. That could mean Couch will be released.

## CAUSES OF CRIMINAL ACTIVITY

Several factors contributed to the growth of the crime rate during the twentieth century. Poverty and broken homes are two major contributors to juvenile crime. During the Great Depression in the 1930s, most families struggled financially. People were accustomed to getting by with few material goods.

The United States economy thrived in the 1940s and 1950s. By the 1960s, the United States had become a consumer society. People expected to live well and have material things. The 1960s also brought decreased respect for authority, especially among young people.

The **complexion** of cities also changed over time. Pockets of deep poverty became firmly **entrenched** in most major cities, and they continued to grow larger. Increasing numbers of youth—especially minority youth—found themselves with few opportunities to get a good education, a good job, or a piece of the American dream. Some of them became involved in gangs; others turned to drugs.

In the 1980s, a crack cocaine **epidemic** swept across the United States. Crack is a solid form of cocaine that could be smoked. Inexpensive and highly addictive, crack snared millions of users, including many teens. By 1985, nearly six million people admitted using cocaine on a routine basis. Increased levels of drug addiction led to increased crime rates among juveniles as teens turned to crime to fuel their drug habits.

Recently, researchers have identified another surprising yet simple factor that may contribute to teen delinquency—lack of sleep. Researchers found that many teens reported feeling drowsy in the afternoon. Those who did tended to exhibit more antisocial behavior such as lying, cheating, stealing, and fighting. A 2017 study by researchers at the University of Pennsylvania and the University of York in the United Kingdom found similar results. Tired teens are 4.5 times more likely to commit violent crimes over the next decade and a half. Professor Adrian Raine of the University of Pennsylvania notes that daytime drowsiness may indicate poor attention. If teens'

Recent research suggests that lack of sleep may contribute to teen crime.

brains are not functioning effectively, they don't think clearly. This makes them more likely to engage in criminal behavior.

## THE TOP FIVE CRIMES

According to the nonprofit Global Youth Justice organization, here are the top five offenses that are referred to Youth Justice **Diversion** Programs:

1. Theft/**Larceny**: Theft/larceny includes shoplifting, stealing from backpacks, or stealing a bicycle.
2. Vandalism: This typically involves damaging cars or spraying graffiti.
3. Alcohol Offenses: Offenses of this nature are related to underage drinking.

4. Disorderly Conduct: Disorderly conduct can cover a wide range of behaviors. Examples include fighting, using obscene or abusive language, making too much noise, or disturbing the peace.
5. Simple Assault or Battery: Simple assault or battery often involves acts such as physical bullying or fighting with a parent.

Other common offenses include possession of marijuana or illegally purchasing tobacco. Traffic violations, truancy, criminal trespass and criminal nuisance, burglary, and possession of a weapon are also among the top twenty-five offenses, according to Global Youth Justice.

# TEEN CRIME IN THE NEWS

The headline "30 Arrested After Flash Mob Strikes Center City Philadelphia" and ones like it dominated the local news in Philadelphia for several days in early March 2017. More than 100 young people ran through the downtown area at rush hour on March 6. Some jumped on cars, and others randomly assaulted bystanders, sending several to the hospital. Ultimately, at least thirty people were arrested.

Crime stories often capture the headlines in both local and national news outlets because those such as murder and rape threaten public safety. Other crimes, when caught on tape like the flash mob was, provide riveting film footage. These crimes seem even more dramatic when committed by teens. The public is shocked to see young people doing horrible things.

News stories often take one of two totally different angles concerning teen crime. One angle portrays a society where teens are out of control. These stories focus on the sensational and violent nature of the crimes. Reporters focus on what needs to be done to regain control. The second angle focuses on the conditions that may have led a teen to commit a crime. Reporters may talk about the teen's broken home life or being bullied or having undiagnosed mental problems.

Some news reports focus on problems within the juvenile justice system. They talk about racial disparity, noting that black and Hispanic teens are far more likely to be arrested and charged with serious crimes than white teens. Reporters also examine the practice of trying juveniles as adults. They debate whether, in the long run, such policies serve the purpose of keeping the public safer. In any case, teen crime will always remain a headline grabber.

A flash mob of thousands, pictured here, caused major gridlock in Philadelphia in 2010. In 2017, another flash mob in the city made headlines. News stories like these shape the public perception of teens.

# CHAPTER TWO

# Teenage Boys in Prison

Seventeen-year-old Demetrius stood silently before the judge, hoping for the best. It wasn't his first time in juvenile court. Even before this arrest, Demetrius had nearly twenty charges on his criminal record. He had been in and out of juvenile centers and juvenile prisons for several years. The only break in his string of troubles came in 2011 when he spent several months in the hospital after being shot. Unable to get around except on crutches while he healed, he stayed out of trouble for nearly a year. Sadly, it didn't last. Roughly half a year later came his armed robbery arrest. Because of Demetrius's age and long criminal record, the judge sent him to Cook County Jail. There he remained for more than three years.

*Opposite*: Boys are far more likely than girls to become part of the juvenile justice system.

Life had always been a challenge for Demetrius. He grew up in a poor neighborhood on Chicago's South Side in a family of seven children being raised by a single mother. Despite having passed eighth grade, he couldn't read, and he couldn't write anything other than his own name. He rarely attended school. When he did, he couldn't sit still.

When he wasn't in trouble, Demetrius and some friends drummed on upside-down buckets in front of public places hoping for donations. He wanted to stay out of trouble. He dreamed of getting a job and helping to take care of his siblings. Unable to read and trapped in a vicious cycle of juvenile crime, he had little chance of making that dream come true.

In many ways, this teen's story, which is featured in Michaela Soyer's book *A Dream Denied: Incarceration, Recidivism, and Young Minority Men in America*, is typical of many male juveniles who find themselves in trouble. Many grow up in poverty and come from broken homes. Many others abuse drugs and become involved with gangs. They find themselves involved with the juvenile justice system time and time again.

Another aspect of Demetrius's story is typical, too. According to 2014 statistics from the Office of Juvenile Justice and Delinquency Prevention, juvenile males are four times more likely to commit violent crimes than juvenile females. Violent crimes include murder, manslaughter, rape, robbery, and aggravated assault.

According to psychologists Martin Daly and Margo Wilson, there are reasons for these statistics. The biggest is that most homicides between men are not planned. Rather, they often start as a relatively minor argument, but because neither man is willing to back down, the situation escalates. Many times it ends in violence, and far too often, someone ends up injured or even dead.

## INFAMOUS EXAMPLES OF MALE TEEN CRIMINALS

Male juvenile delinquency is hardly new, and some of the most notorious criminals in United States history have been juvenile males. William H. Bonney, better known as Billy the Kid, began his criminal career as a sixteen-year-old by stealing food, clothing, and firearms. After escaping from jail, he joined a gang of cattle rustlers. While still a teen, he was involved in several murders before being fatally shot by a sheriff at the age of twenty-one.

Bonnie Parker and Clyde Barrow ranked among the most famous criminals in the United States in the early 1930s. Their spree of bank robberies and killings across Texas drew nationwide attention. Clyde's criminal career began as a teen when he started robbing stores and stealing cars. A stint in Eastham Prison Farm left him a hardened criminal, and after his parole in 1932, he formed his notorious gang. One of his goals was to get back at the Texas criminal system.

Nineteen-year-old mass murderer Charles Starkweather killed ten people in a two-month, two-state crime spree in the mid-1950s. His crime spree drew added attention because of his fascination with "bad boy" movie star James Dean. Starkweather copied the actor's look and style. He and his young accomplice, Caril Ann Fugate, were arrested after a high-speed police chase. Starkweather was executed, and Fugate served many years in prison.

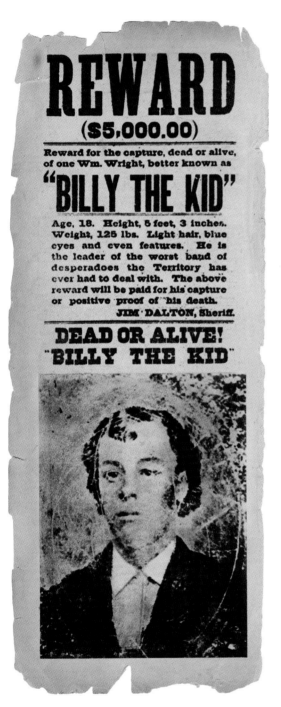

# REWARD

## ($5,000.00)

Reward for the capture, dead or alive, of one Wm. Wright, better known as

## "BILLY THE KID"

Age, 18. Height, 5 feet, 3 inches. Weight, 125 lbs. Light hair, blue eyes and even features. He is the leader of the worst band of desperadoes the Territory has ever had to deal with. The above reward will be paid for his capture or positive proof of his death.

JIM DALTON, Sheriff.

### DEAD OR ALIVE!
### "BILLY THE KID"

Besides crime, these juvenile lawbreakers had something else in common. Their stories all became part of popular culture. For instance, Fugate and Starkweather's crime spree later served as the basis for the movie *Natural Born Killers*. These infamous examples demonstrate a sad fact. Popular culture often glamorizes violence, but the day-to-day realities of teens who break the law are as far from glamorous as you can get.

## GUYS IN GANGS

One factor that leads to juvenile violence is involvement in gangs. Statistics show that juvenile males are more likely to join gangs than

More than a century after his death, outlaw Billy the Kid still ranks as one of the most notorious young criminals in US history.

juvenile females. Although exact figures are hard to determine, statistics suggest that at least three out of every four gang members in the United States is male. One 2010 study places the figure at more than nine out of ten. Males tend to join gangs at a later age than females, and they remain members longer. According to statistics from the National Gang Center, about one in three gang members is age seventeen or under.

Teens who join gangs tend to get involved in drug selling and drug use. They are also likely to get caught up in violent activities. Some of the violence stems from drug trafficking, but fights come from turf wars among rival gangs, too. In fact, it is estimated that more than half of all homicides in Chicago are gang-related.

Chicago and Los Angeles rank as the two top cities for gang activity in the United States. In 2012, ABC News profiled gang life in Chicago. The story described CeaseFire, a program that uses highly trained violence interrupters (often former gang members) to target small groups of high-risk individuals in violent neighborhoods. The goal is to try to mediate conflicts before they end in violence.

ABC News also interviewed five gang members about their involvement. Michael described the beating he absorbed from fellow gang members when he joined at age thirteen. "You got to take a beat down … just to show them you're tough," he said. He added that the gang was as much a part of his family as his mother and sister. Damien got involved with gangs when was just nine years old. By the age of twenty-eight, he had been arrested more than fifty times, and he survived being hit by six gunshots while leaving a party in a rival gang's neighborhood.

Despite everything, Damien still felt a strong attraction to gang life. He summed up the reasons that many young people turn to gangs, saying, "I had no guidance. So I was raised to be knocked on the streets, running around, looking at the older guys, what they had that I didn't have, and I wanted that."

According to a 2013 study in the United Kingdom, most juveniles who participate in gangs suffer from some kind of psychiatric illness. In fact, gang members are four times as likely to suffer from psychosis as teens in general. More than half of gang members also suffer from alcohol or drug dependency. Jeremy Coid, director of the Forensic Psychiatry Research Unit at Queen Mary University and lead author of the paper, said that the research identifies "a complex public

Statistically, boys face a much greater risk of joining gangs than girls do.

health problem at the intersection of violence, substance misuse, and mental health problems among young men."

## MENTAL HEALTH ISSUES

Mental health issues play a role in as many as 65 percent to 70 percent of all juvenile arrests, according to a report from the National Conference of State Legislatures. One in four of those arrested suffers from a mental illness so severe that it impairs the teen's ability to function normally. Furthermore, a majority of youth in the juvenile justice system who have diagnosable psychiatric disorders also have a substance abuse disorder.

Mental health issues affect both males and females. In fact, studies indicate that female offenders demonstrate higher rates of mental health symptoms than males. Another study, however, focused on mental health issues as they relate to serious juvenile crimes. Males commit the vast majority of those crimes; therefore, they made up roughly five out of six of the study subjects.

The analysis found some interesting results. Adolescent offenders with mental health problems did not show higher levels of re-arrest or self-reported antisocial activity. What did make a difference was substance abuse. Teens with substance abuse disorders showed higher rates of re-arrest, self-reported antisocial activity, and less time spent productively than other offenders. Coupled with other mental health issues, substance abuse appears to contribute to increased risk of reoffending or antisocial behavior.

## BOYS AT RISK

Boys already start out at a much higher risk of committing juvenile crime than females. Some other factors put certain males at even greater risk. The first is race. As noted earlier, African Americans and Hispanics are far more likely to be arrested for juvenile crimes than whites. Part of the problem is that young African Americans and Hispanics are more likely to have other factors that put them at risk. For one thing, black and Hispanic youth are more likely to live in high-poverty sections of cities. This puts them in areas where gangs tend to be more active and drug use is more widespread.

But there is another factor at play as well—a sort of chicken and egg type situation. Statistics show that the highest crime rates take place in certain high-poverty areas of cities. Therefore, police tend to patrol those areas more frequently. Since more black and Hispanic youth live in these neighborhoods, they find themselves under more surveillance, regardless of whether they are engaged in criminal activity.

Some might call this racial profiling. Others might argue that it simply represents police officers reacting to known statistics and trends. Another question relates to how officers react in situations surrounding black or Hispanic teens who are accused of a crime.

## EQUAL TREATMENT?

Certainly, many African Americans and Hispanics feel they are unfairly targeted by police officers and others who automatically view them as suspicious, and race appears to have played a role in several high-profile cases involving teens. In February 2012, seventeen-year-old Trayvon Martin was shot and killed by George Zimmerman in Sanford, Florida. Zimmerman, a neighborhood watch captain in the gated Retreat at Twin Lakes community, thought Martin looked suspicious. He followed Martin and at some point confronted the youth. An altercation followed. Charged with manslaughter, Zimmerman said he fired his gun in self-defense; a jury found him innocent.

On August 9, 2014, in Ferguson, Missouri, a white police officer named Darren Wilson fatally shot eighteen-year-old Michael Brown. Brown had allegedly robbed a nearby convenience store. Eyewitness accounts varied as to exactly what happened when Wilson tried to arrest Brown. Some witnesses said Brown charged the officer. Others said he tried to surrender. In either case, Wilson fired twelve shots at the teen, killing him. No charges were brought against Wilson.

On November 22, 2014, police in Cleveland, Ohio, responded to a report of man with a gun in a local park. The dispatcher failed to inform the responding officers that the person in question was a juvenile and that the gun he was holding was probably not real. As the officers approached twelve-year-old Tamir Rice, he reached toward his waistband. One of the officers fired twice, fatally wounding the boy. The gun was later found to be an air pellet gun. A grand jury declined to indict the police officer who fired the fatal shot, though a lawsuit brought by the boy's family against the city of Cleveland was later settled for $6 million.

In February 2017, an off-duty Los Angeles police officer got into a confrontation with a group of teens at his home in Anaheim. He said the teens trespassed on his property. He grabbed one teen by the shirt, and another teen charged the

Twelve-year-old Tamir Rice was shot and killed by police officers in Cleveland in 2014.

man and knocked him over. The officer pulled out a gun and fired. The teens scattered, and no one was injured. Some of the teens appeared to be Latino; the officer was white. The incident sparked protests, and more than twenty protesters were arrested.

Incidents like these and others make some people question whether there really is justice in juvenile justice. Critics believe that minorities are targeted by police, regardless of whether they are actually committing an offense. They also believe that police treat minorities differently than they would treat white teens in arrest situations.

## JUVENILES IN ADULT PRISONS

Life in a juvenile detention facility can be challenging. However, teens assigned there can consider themselves lucky compared to those sentenced to serve time in adult prisons. On any given day, more than four thousand juveniles in the United States find themselves in adult prisons, according to the nonprofit organization Sentencing Project. Beginning in the 1990s, many states began taking a harsher outlook on crime. According to some social scientists, the United States was creating a generation of violent youth without conscience. Concern grew about so-called super-predators, or young offenders who would commit crimes over and over because they didn't know right from wrong. The fear proved unfounded, as youth crime rates have dropped over the past twenty years.

However, fears about super-predators helped spark a trend that remains today. More and more states now allow teens to be tried as adults. Juvenile cases can be transferred to an adult court through a procedure known as a waiver. As a result, increasing numbers of teens are being sentenced to serve time in adult prisons.

Teens can't vote until they turn eighteen. They can't get a tattoo without parental permission, and they can't buy cigarettes. Likewise, most states treat offenders under the age of eighteen as juveniles, and these states try the offenders in juvenile courts. If the offenders are sentenced to detention, they serve that detention in a juvenile facility. In a few states, however,

On any given day, more than four thousand juveniles in the US find themselves in adult prisons such as this one.

sixteen- or seventeen-year-old offenders are likely to be tried as adults. If sentenced, they will be sent to adult prisons.

Sometimes, juveniles as young as twelve are tried as adults. This typically occurs only in murder cases. In some cases, juveniles this young have been sentenced to life in prison without the possibility of parole. Until a Supreme Court ruling in 2005 prohibiting it, juveniles could even be sentenced to death.

Young people sentenced to life in prison without parole could conceivably spend seventy years or more behind bars. According to The Sentencing Project, approximately 2,500 juveniles are currently serving such sentences. In many cases, these sentences were mandatory based on the crime. This means that the judge had no leeway to consider the offender's age during sentencing.

The 2012 US Supreme Court ruling in *Miller v. Alabama* changed that. The ruling required states and the federal government to consider the unique situations of each juvenile defendant, saying that giving juveniles a mandatory life sentence without the possibility of parole is unconstitutional. Provisions need to be made for offenders who show that they have been rehabilitated while in prison.

As a result of this ruling, states are reviewing the cases of juveniles who received such mandatory sentences. Many people consider this a social justice issue, though there are also practical considerations. Housing juveniles in prison for decades costs a lot of money. In fact, The Sentencing Project estimates the cost of keeping an offender in prison for fifty years is approximately $2.25 million.

Needless to say, adult prisons present a far harsher experience than juvenile facilities. In juvenile detention

# A DAY IN THE LIFE AT A JUVENILE DETENTION CENTER

The daily routine for a male teen prisoner in a juvenile facility varies from state to state and from facility to facility. Here's what a day could look like, based on a day at the detention center in Clallam County, Washington:

A loud buzzer wakes the prisoners. At 7:00 a.m. the locked door to their rooms open. Doors to other rooms throughout the pod open as well. Sleepy figures stumble into the hall, and they walk single file toward the breakfast area, passing through electronically secured doors on the way. Prisoners are not allowed to speak as they walk. Breaking the rules can cause them to lose privileges—they may lose the right to see movies or play sports during their free time. Free-time activities represent one of the few choices these teens enjoy, so they try hard not to lose those activities.

After breakfast, the teens briefly return to their rooms. School starts promptly at 8:30. Again, the teens exit their cells and pass through several secure doors before reaching their classroom. School runs 8:30 to 3:00 each day. The teens get a brief break around mid-morning and another at lunchtime. After school, the teens have "free time," though they remain confined to their own pod during this time. They may make phone calls or watch movies. To make a call, teens must call collect on a supervised phone; if they watch a movie, it's a movie that has been selected and approved by the detention center personnel.

The teens return to the cafeteria for an early dinner at 4:30. After dinner, they do homework. They also have to clean their cell each day and take a shower at a designated time. If their behavior has earned them the privilege, they may be able to use the gymnasium or the outdoor yard in the evening.

Home sweet home is a small, sparse room. A single bed sits against one wall. A small metal desk sits in the corner. Each cell has a toilet and sink, and teens usually have a cell to themselves. However, a few cells are designated as doubles and may be used if the prison population demands it.

Visitation rights depend on how severe the teens' offense is and how their behavior has been. Typically, visitations are limited to certain days of the week. In most cases, only parents can visit. Like the teens, the visiting parents must pass through security checkpoints. Visitations take place in the cafeteria where there is no privacy. Not only that, but the teens get patted down at the end of the visit to ensure that their visitors didn't give them any contraband items.

In a juvenile detention center, teens' lives are controlled by others. The days and weeks are pretty much the same. Most teens eagerly count down the days until their release.

Even when teens in a juvenile detention center get time outside, they are constantly reminded that they are confined.

centers, teens are surrounded by other teens. Some may have committed serious crimes, but many are there for lesser offenses. In adult prisons, they might share a cell or cell block with armed robbers, rapists, and murderers.

Imagine how teen offenders feel in such a setting. They live in constant fear of physical or even sexual abuse. They may join a prison gang or turn to a few older inmates for protection. That protection often comes at a price, however. "Putting teens in jails or prisons with adults is a traumatic experience for them," says Marcy Mistrett, CEO of Campaign for Youth Justice. "It's a very scary place. They are subject to predatory behavior from other people."

Furthermore, adult prisons generally offer few opportunities for education or treatment. When they complete their sentence, teens may leave prison as a more hardened criminal than when they entered. Indeed, research shows that teen offenders who serve their time in a juvenile detention facility are more likely to move past delinquency and turn their lives around than those who serve their sentences in an adult prison.

With that in mind, the Justice Policy Institute (JPI) published a report in March 2017 titled "Raising the Age: Shifting to a Safer and More Effective Juvenile Justice System." The report notes that over the past decade, seven states have passed laws raising the age of juvenile court jurisdiction to eighteen. Meanwhile, each of the remaining states that try sixteen- or seventeen-year-olds as adults is considering legislation to raise the age to eighteen.

According to JPI, some of the states that recently raised the age of juvenile court jurisdiction initially feared that the move might overwhelm juvenile courts and detention centers.

Instead, juvenile rates continue to fall. Supporters believe that extending juvenile jurisdiction contributes to this trend by helping more teen offenders get the education and treatment they need to move past delinquency.

## LIFE AFTER PRISON

What happens to male teens after serving time in a juvenile detention center depends on several factors. These include the juvenile's home life, their educational status, and their experience while incarcerated. Juveniles who return to loving, supportive homes often are able to put the detention experience behind them and start again. Those who return to broken homes or abusive parents often return to the juvenile justice system again and again.

The same holds true with education. Teens with solid academic skills often can slide right back into the routine of their school. Those who struggle to learn find themselves even further behind than when they left. They often tune out or even drop out.

Juveniles' futures are also shaped by their experiences while serving time. For some, incarceration represents a bottoming out. Arrested for assault as a teen, singer/actor Mark Wahlberg credits the forty-five days he spent in prison with turning his life around. "When I went to jail, that was a wake-up call," he later said. Wahlberg sought help and went on to achieve a successful career.

Other teens learn all the wrong things while incarcerated. They may meet other teens who are experienced criminals and might learn new ideas about crime that they will try out on their own when released. Any self-discipline they may have picked up during their detention quickly disappears. They go on to become repeat offenders. The tendency to slip back into criminal ways is known as recidivism.

No one knows for sure how many teens return to lives of crime after encountering the juvenile justice system. According to a 2014 report funded by the OJJDP, "There is no national recidivism rate for juveniles. Each state's juvenile justice system differs in organization, administration, and data capacity." Furthermore, each state defines and measures recidivism differently.

# SCARED STRAIGHT

In 1978, the film *Scared Straight* documented at-risk youth who had been in trouble with the law visiting an adult prison in Rahway, New Jersey. There they saw what life in prison would be like. They met hardened convicts who described the bad choices they made that led to their imprisonment. The convicts yelled at and threatened the teens, hoping to scare them into better behavior.

*Scared Straight* won the Academy Award for Best Documentary Feature in 1978. But did it work? A follow up twenty years later found that only two of the seventeen teens who had experienced prison life went on to lead lives of crimes. The others managed to stay "straight," and they credited their visit to prison with helping them turn things around.

Beginning in 2009, *Beyond Scared Straight* began airing on the A&E network. Each episode took a different set of teens in different states to experience life behind bars. Over the next several years, the program featured more than three hundred teens visiting prisons in twenty-nine states. Now some states run their own Scared Straight programs. Others run boot camps or other programs that offer a similar experience.

Opinions vary on how effective these programs are. Proponents say the programs really do scare teens into turning their lives around. Critics say that once the shock wears off, many teens fall back into criminal behavior.

The film *Scared Straight* took troubled teens into Rahway State Prison to get a taste of life behind bars.

# CHAPTER THREE

# Teenage Girls in Prison

Elizabeth, eighteen, described her younger self as a "chronic runaway." She told a reporter from *L.A. Youth* that she had been in various juvenile placement facilities since fifth grade. She said she began running away after her stepfather molested her, and after he died, her mother's new boyfriend threatened her with a knife, so she ran away again. "They arrested me on a runaway charge," she recalled. "Nothing happened to him. I had good grades, all A's and stuff like that, but I just couldn't take being in school, so I dropped out."

The hardest thing about being incarcerated was losing her freedom. In addition, she felt all alone—her family visited her just twice during the year she was there. "It felt like the whole world was going on without me, and I was stuck," Elizabeth said. "It's hard being out here all by yourself. I can see what

*Opposite*: Girls represent the fastest growing segment of the juvenile justice system.

they're doing to us. How kids are sent to jail when they just need a slap on the head or something."

Unfortunately, cases like this occur every night across the United States. Girls make up the fastest growing segment of the juvenile justice system, according to a report from the Georgetown Center on Poverty, Inequality and Public Policy. Furthermore, they represent a "high need" and "low risk" group. This means that although they have many challenges and needs, they do not pose much threat to society. Although boys continue to outnumber girls by more than two to one in the juvenile justice system, the proportion of girls continues to grow.

## A TRAGIC TALE

On October 21, 2009, fifteen-year-old Alyssa Bustamante of Cole County, Missouri, lured her nine-year-old neighbor, Elizabeth Olten, into a nearby wooded area. There she stabbed the girl, strangled her, and slashed her throat. She left the dead girl in a shallow grave and covered the body with leaves. Bustamante's motive: she just wanted to know what it felt like to kill someone. She wrote in her diary that she found the experience "pretty enjoyable."

The murder of a young girl by someone who was only a teenager herself sent shock waves through the small community. Bustamante led a troubled life. The product of a broken home with no parent present, she had attempted suicide multiple times. She had cut herself many times and burned herself with cigarettes. One of her social media profiles listed one of her hobbies as "killing people." The case drew nationwide coverage.

Teenager Alyssa Bustamante was sentenced to life in prison for the murder of her nine-year-old neighbor.

Charged with first-degree murder, Bustamante was ordered to stand trial as an adult. Shortly before the trial was to begin, she pleaded guilty to a lesser charge of second-degree murder. Just before her sentencing, she said: "If I could give my life to bring her back, I would." The judge sentenced her to life in prison, but she does have the possibility of parole at some point.

This terrifying image of a teenage killer, murdering for the thrill of it, typifies how many people view juvenile criminals. The profile of the typical teen female criminal, however, is far different—and far less frightening.

## TRENDS AND FIGURES

Juvenile crime in general has been dropping over the past twenty years. According to FBI statistics, the total number of arrests for youth under eighteen years of age dropped from 1.45 million to 1.24 million between 2000 and 2009. The number of arrests for boys dropped by 22.9 percent over that decade. The decline for girls was somewhat less, at 13.1 percent. The number of juvenile arrests per year has continued to drop since then. In 2015, it stood at roughly 920,000. That represents a drop of about one-third from 2006.

One big difference between girls and boys in the juvenile system is the types of crimes that bring them there. Boys often find themselves under arrest for violent crimes such as murder, rape, or robbery. Girls account for only about 10 percent of juvenile arrests in these categories. Still, the number of girls arrested for robbery between 2000 and 2009 rose by more than 30 percent. Most girls, however, have been arrested for nonviolent crimes. By far, the most common reason for arrest among girls is larceny. Larceny, which includes shoplifting, accounts for more than one out of every four arrests of juvenile females. Drug abuse violations are also common, accounting for nearly seventeen thousand female arrests in 2009.

Furthermore, girls often find themselves in the juvenile justice system for status offenses. For example, more than thirty-two thousand females were arrested for running away in 2009. That makes running away the most common status offense leading to females being arrested.

## COMMON CHARACTERISTICS AND DIFFERENCES FROM BOYS

While females may commit different offenses from males, they do share some common characteristics. Like boys, many of the girls who enter the juvenile justice system live in poverty-stricken homes. Many have endured abuse. They live trapped in a nightmarish present with little hope for a better future. Lack of opportunity may lead them to steal. Lack of hope may lead them to drink, abuse drugs, or run away from home.

As with boys, there are far more young women of color in juvenile detention facilities than one would expect based on population demographics. According to figures from OJJDP, black females are 20 percent more likely to be detained than white females. American Indian girls are 50 percent more likely to be detained. LGBTQ youth also find themselves twice as likely to be arrested and convicted than heterosexual girls who had committed similar offenses. If sent to a juvenile detention center, LGBTQ youth are far more likely to be victims of violence.

Girls are far more likely than boys to have been sexually abused. In eight out of ten sexual abuse cases, the victim is female. A study of girls in juvenile correctional settings conducted by the American Correctional Association in 1990 yielded some alarming findings. More than half of the girls (54.3 percent) had experienced sexual abuse in their lives. Furthermore, more than half of them had suffered such abuse multiple times.

A study of juvenile girls at a facility in California found similar results. Three out of four (74 percent) reported being hurt or in danger of being hurt at home. Six in ten (60 percent) reported being raped or in danger of being raped at some point in their lives. A similar study in Florida yielded similar results. Two out of three girls (64 percent) reported past abuse. With such traumatic upbringings, it's not surprising that these girls find themselves pulled into dangerous or illegal behaviors. It's also not surprising that many had resorted to running away in an attempt to escape bad situations.

## A LITTLE HISTORY

As with boys, the beginning of juvenile centers for girls came around 1900 as part of the Progressive movement. However, the goals were quite different. The main reason for sending boys to reform schools was to prevent them from becoming criminals. On the other hand, reformers sent girls to reform school to prevent them from becoming "wayward." Basically, this means out of control. In reality, it referred to preventing girls from doing activities that were considered improper for unmarried girls.

As a result of this attitude, girls received much harsher treatment in court than boys. In Chicago, half of delinquent girls were sent to reformatories. Only one in five delinquent boys received similar sentences. Statistics from several other cities showed similar trends. This type of treatment continued into the middle of the twentieth century. Far different from today, roughly seven out of ten girls brought in for delinquency were white. Today, African Americans and Hispanics are found in disproportionate numbers.

In 1950, more than three out of four girls referred to juvenile court in Los Angeles were charged with status offenses. But the nature of the offenses had changed. By 1950, fewer girls drew charges of "waywardness" or "immorality." Instead, most faced charges of running away, truancy, or curfew violation. Still, roughly half were charged with sexual misconduct. In many states, girls who were referred to the juvenile justice system for status offenses were more likely to be placed in an institution than boys who were referred for felony offenses.

The Juvenile Justice and Delinquency Prevention Act of 1974 changed all that. The act called for states to move toward deinstitutionalization for status offenders. As a result, the percentage of girls incarcerated began to drop. It peaked around 34 percent in 1950. By 1990, it had dropped to 11 percent. Then it began to trend upward again. In 2006, girls represented 22 percent of detention admissions.

The 1992 reauthorization of the JJDP brought another key change. For the first time, the law made specific reference to providing services especially designed for girls. Special challenge grants encouraged states to examine how they were treating girls. It also encouraged them to set up programs designed to meet the needs of females.

Most juvenile boys committed to detention earn their way there by committing serious offenses. The same does not hold true for girls. Girls continue to be far more likely than boys to be arrested and sentenced to confinement for status crimes such as running away and curfew violations. Furthermore, girls are far more likely to experience **bootstrapping** than boys. Bootstrapping involves adding charges to a single criminal incident. For instance, a girl who runs away might get probation. In addition, a court order says she must not run away again. If she does, she faces two charges. She faces the charge of running away, but she also faces a **contempt of court** charge for violating the rules of her probation. The two charges together might cause her to be sentenced to time in a juvenile detention center.

In some cases, the judge might feel that this sentence will protect the young person. It prevents her from having to immediately return to an unstable home situation. It might even protect her from physical or sexual abuse. On the other hand, being detained in a juvenile detention center places her among a group of other offenders. Some may have committed serious crimes. Spending time locked up with such people may push her toward a life of crime herself.

## GENDER-SPECIFIC TREATMENT

The Juvenile Justice and Delinquency Prevention Act of 1992 instructed states to provide "gender-specific" treatment to female offenders. Ever since, states have wrestled with how to do so effectively. In recent years, a number of researchers have focused on the best practices for helping young females.

In 2010, researchers D. A. Andrews and James Bonta addressed this issue in the fifth edition of their book *The Psychology of Criminal Conduct*. They identified several factors as being effective in working with females: women-only groups, individual sessions with a female helper, staff modeling of healthy relationships, creation of a community with a sense of connection, emphasis on safety, emphasis on connecting, mutual respect, building on strengths, emphasis on raising and exploring issues, and treatment within the least restrictive environment.

In analyzing this and other research regarding juvenile female offenders, the Utah Criminal Justice Center developed the following recommendations, which they believe can best serve female offenders and reduce recidivism:

1. As with male offenders, the highest risk female offenders should receive the most intensive services.
2. Treatment should target **criminogenic** needs, or risk factors or characteristics that relate to likelihood of recidivism.
3. Treatment should include strategies such as modeling, reinforcement, role playing, skill building, cognitive restructuring, and the learning (and repeated practicing) of low-risk behaviors in high-risk situations.
4. The unique qualities of females should be addressed.
5. In addition to targeting criminogenic needs, curricula should also include offenders in groups that target other needs. For instance, these groups might address self-esteem, self-expression, and trauma.

However, despite reforms, few facilities are designed specifically to house female juveniles. This means that girls are often sent to facilities far from their homes. In other cases, they are placed in facilities that are not well equipped to meet their needs.

## STATES TAKE ACTION

Gradually, however, states are making progress. Both Connecticut and Florida have worked to better serve the needs of females in the juvenile justice system. Their initiatives have some common elements. Both stress the

# C. J.'S STORY

Each day, juvenile courts across the United States hear more than 4,600 cases, according to statistics from the FBI. In most of these cases, a judge listens to the evidence and renders a decision; very rarely does a jury participate. On any given day, a judge might hear cases involving runaways, drug sellers, car thieves, and juveniles charged with assault. Sometimes the most serious cases get transferred to adult courts. There they receive full jury trials.

Most cases, however, involve less serious offenses. Many revolve around low-grade crimes such as shoplifting or petty theft. According to a case study from PRIME Education, fourteen-year-old C. J. ran away from home to escape a troubled home situation. She thought she could make it on her own. But when the little bit of money she had ran out, she had to steal in order to feed herself. Arrested for petty theft, she found herself in juvenile court.

C. J. was lucky. The judge sentenced her to six months in a teen residential center. There she got help addressing her problems. The center housed twenty juvenile girls between the ages of eleven and eighteen. They came from different backgrounds, but they had many things in common. Many came from unstable

A teenage girl gets her day in court.

families. Some were dealing with drug and alcohol abuse problems. Others had faced verbal, physical, or even sexual abuse. Their illegal behavior often stemmed from an inability to manage anger or deal with the difficult situations in their lives.

Once at the center, C. J. signed a contract presented by the center's behavioral health case manager. During the six months she was there, C. J. learned to bring order and structure to her life. She worked hard and knew that if she failed she might end up with a more severe punishment. As time went on, C. J. gradually learned to regulate her behaviors and make better choices. Only time will tell if C. J. will be able to maintain her progress in the outside world.

importance of collaboration among multiple government agencies and community-based organizations. In addition, both place an emphasis on training juvenile justice personnel in gender-responsive approaches. Connecticut has also passed legislation that prohibits the detention of status offenders.

Florida has found success in supporting diversion programs. The nonprofit PACE Center for Girls has become nationally recognized for its success in helping at-risk girls turn their lives around. Founded in 1985 with a single center, PACE now runs nineteen nonresidential centers across Florida. Formed as an alternative to institutionalization or incarceration for girls, the centers provide a mix of academics and social services to help middle school and high school girls achieve success in academics and throughout their lives. The PACE Center serves two thousand girls a year.

Connecticut lawmakers have passed laws to help young female offenders. Pictured is the Connecticut State Capitol.

Felicia Wriley currently works as a program assistant for PACE Broward. A former PACE student herself, she attests to the power of the program to change lives. "In addition to PACE saving my soul, the skills I learned while enrolled in the program strengthened my bond with my family and gave me the tools necessary to evolve into the woman I am today," Wriley says.

## LIFE AFTER INCARCERATION

As with boys, a girl's life after incarceration depends on many factors. Most important is probably the home life she returns to. Many more girls than boys are placed in detention for status offenses such as running away from home or arguing with parents. Girls who run away often come from broken homes. Many have been physically or sexually abused. Returning to such situations raises the chances that girls will once again find themselves in the juvenile justice system. On the other hand, many girls who come from stable homes are able to turn their lives around. Being in detention convinces them to change their behavior; they leave incarceration determined to make a fresh start.

The success that girls find after incarceration also depends on the quality of the detention program. Programs that focus on the specific needs of girls tend to have better results; so do smaller, treatment-oriented programs. Such programs can help reduce the recidivism rate and ensure that fewer girls become repeat offenders.

# GIRLS IN GANGS

Eighteen-year-old Tayshana Murphy of Harlem seemingly had a great life ahead of her. The highly rated basketball player had received a scholarship to Miami University. A career in the WBNA looked likely. It all ended in a heartbeat. On September 11, 2011, Murphy was gunned down as part of a dispute between rival gangs.

Although the vast majority of gang members across the United States are male, many girls participate as well. Some become members of predominately male gangs. Others join all-female gangs. In 2006, just 1 percent of girls reported that they belonged to a gang, compared to 3 percent of boys. This would suggest that about one of four gang members across the United States is female. A survey by the National Gang Center found a much lower number. That survey found that just 7.4 percent of all gang members were females. But researchers agree that it is difficult to report figures on gang participation. That said, we know that girls tend to join gangs at a younger age than boys. They also tend to leave the gangs once they reach their mid to upper teens. Boys, on the other hand, often remain in gangs into their late teens and beyond.

Like boys, many girls join gangs seeking protection and acceptance. Others use gang participation as an escape from a troubled home life. "Sometimes the act of joining a gang is experienced as empowerment," said gang researcher Meda Chesney-Lind of the University of Hawaii in a 2012 *Huffington Post* article. "It doesn't really matter if it's a male gang or a female gang—all that matters is the feeling of control."

Teenage girls join gangs seeking protection, acceptance, escape, and empowerment.

CHAPTER FOUR

# Economic Prisoners

Not all prisons have bars. Millions of teens, especially in low-income countries, are prisoners of an economic system that forces them to go work at an early age. These working conditions sometimes closely resemble the confinement of a prison. Teenagers in the United States, Europe, and other high-income countries have the opportunity to attend school through most of their teen years. Most graduate from high school, and many go on to college. When they finish their education, they have a variety of job options.

Teenagers in some developing areas of the world are far less fortunate. They have to work to help support their families. Working is not necessarily a bad thing for young people, as long as it does not endanger their health or prevent their education. Many teens around the world, however, work in dangerous

*Opposite*: In many areas of the world, teens work at difficult and sometimes dangerous jobs, like this young man working on a cocoa farm in Ghana.

conditions. Some labor underground in dark, cramped mines. Others pick through trash in large cities looking for something to sell. Some are virtual prisoners, shackled to looms in mills. They are not set loose until their shift ends. They often work ten or twelve hours each day. Those who are forced to sit or stand at a loom all day may have even less physical freedom than a teen in an actual prison.

## A WORLDWIDE PROBLEM

According to the International Labour Organization (ILO), there were more than 168 million child laborers worldwide in 2012. The ILO defines child labor as work "that deprives children of their childhood, their potential, and their dignity, and that is harmful to physical and mental development." The definition covers children who are between five and seventeen years of age.

Work often deprives children of the chance to attend school. The Global Partnership for Education estimates that 121 million children and adolescents are currently out of primary and lower secondary school worldwide. Nearly half of these children (55 million) live in sub-Saharan Africa. Children who do not get an education lose the opportunity to get ahead. They often remain trapped in low-paying manual labor jobs throughout their entire lives.

In some countries, poverty-stricken families face a difficult choice. They may realize that their children need an education in order to have a better life. They want their children to have that opportunity. But often they themselves hold low-paying jobs. They struggle to pay the rent on a tiny home and put food on the table. They need the meager income that their children can generate to make ends meet.

The situation hits girls hardest. More girls than boys are left out of primary school and lower secondary school. There are several reasons for this, including the fact that some families do not place a high value on the education of girls. They might understand that, over time, girls who are educated have opportunities to gain better jobs and earn more money. Often, however, families need immediate economic support. Sending a teenage girl to school represents a long-term investment, and the family won't see the economic benefits for several years. Sending that same teenage girl to work helps meet the family's immediate needs; often those immediate needs win out. But the teenage girl loses, not just over the short term but over her entire life. Without an education, girls end up working in low-paying jobs with little hope of bettering themselves.

This issue hits close to home, even in developed countries. A quick check of the labels on common items that US teenagers use or wear reveals that many of them are made in developing countries—often by other teens. Teenagers in Bangladesh stitch together the soccer balls that teenagers in the United States use in their soccer leagues. Teenagers in Uzbekistan pick the cotton used to make blue jeans. Teenagers in India may spin the cotton into yarn and then factory workers in India, Bangladesh, or China may stitch the yarn into jeans. Often the young workers in these various factories make just pennies per hour.

## LURED BY FALSE PROMISES

Often teenagers work because they need to help support their family. In other cases, they are lured to work by false promises. In India, garment factory owners sometimes promise teenage girls good wages, a decent place to live, and the chance for further education. Once they arrive, the girls find a far different situation. They work twelve- to fourteen-hour days spinning cotton into yarn. They lived crowded together in tiny rooms owned by the factory. They receive far lower wages than promised, and they have no chance for education.

Once in such a situation, teens find it difficult to leave. They are far from home, with no easy way to get back to their families. And the wages they earn, although small, are at least something. Some teens have no option to leave. They have been signed into **bonded labor**. This bond requires them to work for a specific term (often three to five years) at a fixed wage. They have to live in company-owned camps or hostels. They are rarely allowed to leave the company compound. In many ways, the conditions resemble those of a prison. These teens have committed no crime, yet they live in prison-like conditions for several years. The end of their bonded period can even be compared to the end of a prison sentence.

ILO Convention 138 allows developing countries to set the minimum working age at fourteen years. However, requiring children of that age to work long hours or night shifts would violate the rules. Most countries worldwide have ratified this convention. A few, including the United States, Australia, New Zealand, India, Bangladesh, and Myanmar, have not. In the United States, Australia, and New Zealand, it's not an issue.

Girls working in garment factories in some countries may be forced to work twelve- to fourteen-hour shifts.

In India, Bangladesh, and Myanmar, factory owners often take advantage of young workers.

A report by the Fair Labor Association in 2012 described how a number of international garment manufacturers took advantage of young female workers under the Sumangali system. Under this scheme, mill representatives recruit young women from poor rural areas of India to work as "apprentices" in spinning mills. Two out of three girls recruited were between the ages of twelve and sixteen.

The girls are promised a lump sum payment at the end of three years. They also are promised a monthly stipend. They are told that they will live in a hostel, and the modest cost of their lodging and meals will be deducted from their wages. In theory, the practice could work because the mills get steady labor and the girls earn money toward marriage. In some areas of India, a girl's family needs to provide a dowry—or cash payment—in order for her to get married, and the factory work could help the girls raise that money. In fact, "Sumangali" means "happily married woman."

In practice, some mill owners abused the system. They forced the girls to work long hours and provided poor working and living conditions. They paid the girls lower wages than they promised, and they deducted unfair amounts for "room and board." In some cases, they prevented the girls from leaving the factory grounds. Many people thought this violated the workers' rights. These conditions seemed more like a prison than a workplace. Even if the girls were physically free to leave, they probably had no means—or money—to travel home. They were trapped in a sentence of work that was not unlike a prison sentence.

## EXPOSING ABUSE

A report by the Fair Labor Association looked at the cases of seventy-eight girls in different factories. Quite a few of them failed to finish their three-year terms. Four died from accident or illness. Eleven left because of health problems. Nineteen others were taken home by their parents or left on their own. Of the seventy-eight, only twenty-four had completed their contracts. Twenty were still working at the time of the survey.

A book titled *Modeslavar*, or *Fashion Slaves*, published in Sweden in 2015, tells how girls as young as fourteen work twelve-hour days to make clothing for name-brand companies. In 2015, the rights organization Oxfam reported on conditions in twenty-two factories in Myanmar. Some young workers reported working all night to meet a clothing deadline. Others said they were treated "like animals."

Oxfam noted that 90 percent of the young workers in these factories were young women. They earned as little as $0.60 a day for their labor. In many cases, they worked long overtime shifts, which they were forced to accept. They also faced high production targets and verbal abuse from their supervisors.

Some consumers may decide that they don't want to wear clothing made by teenage workers who work for substandard wages in abusive conditions. But that's not always easy to determine. There are thousands of clothing factories in countries such as India, Bangladesh, Pakistan, and Myanmar. Some treat workers more fairly than others. The supply chain for clothing is long and complex. It spans multiple continents, and so it can be hard to tell where a piece of clothing was originally made.

Some major companies have tried to improve conditions in the countries in which their products are made. But even they have trouble enforcing fair labor guidelines. Factories have become highly skilled at hiding violations when inspectors visit. It's a problem with no easy solution.

## A CLOSER LOOK AT EXPLOITATION

Young girls are not alone in facing exploitation in the workplace. It happens to boys, too. In some cases, the exploitation reaches nearly slave-like proportions. In Senegal, thousands of children, most of them boys, are sent to study with a spiritual guide. Instead, in some cases the guides force them to beg on the streets. The guides keep all the money the children earn. In many cases the boys are prisoners. They depend on the guides for food and shelter, and even if they could escape, they have no way to get home. Similar experiences are found in several industries around the world.

## MINE WORKERS

Meanwhile, as many as one million children in Africa, Asia, Latin America, and America are forced to work in mines and quarries. According to the Human Rights Council, children as young as three years old serve as virtual slaves. They may be restricted from leaving company property, and they are forced to depend on their employer for food and shelter. Like the boys in Senegal, these children have no way out. Worsening the problem, workers in the mines and quarries risk injury each day, and they often grow ill from inhaling rock dust.

## COCOA FARMERS

Almost everyone loves chocolate, but not the young children who are forced to work long hours under horrible conditions on cocoa farms. An estimated 500,000 children—most of them boys—work in the cocoa fields in Ghana and the Ivory Coast. More than half of the world's cocoa is produced there. This means that beans for much of the chocolate candy consumed in the United States have been picked by child laborers. Many of these young workers are orphans or homeless. CNN talked to a ten-year-old on an Ivory Coast who had been working for three years. He said he was not allowed to leave the farm or go to school, and he wasn't paid. He was not just an economic prisoner; he was a physical prisoner. Sadly, thousands of other young workers live in similar conditions.

## CHILD SOLDIERS

In some war-torn countries, children and teens are forced to become soldiers. They work for the older soldiers with no hope of escape. Children age ten or younger may even be forced to carry weapons. Most of these forced soldiers are boys, although

In war-torn countries, children and teens are sometimes forced into becoming soldiers. Here, a boy serves as a soldier in Afghanistan.

sometimes girls are pressed into fighting as well. Sometimes they have watched loved ones killed in brutal attacks.

For instance, during the Sierra Leone civil war, children who fled terror from one side of the fighting were captured and enslaved by the opposing side. They were given weapons and their captors made them shoot other children who tried to escape.

## DANGEROUS AND DEADLY

According to the International Labour Organization, an estimated 85 million youth between the ages of five and seventeen do what is considered hazardous work. Each day they are exposed to conditions that put their health—and sometimes even their lives—at risk. Most of these young people work in either Asia and the Pacific or sub-Saharan Africa. In sub-Saharan Africa, more than 10 percent of the entire population of children are in this situation. Worldwide, boys face higher risks of being involved in hazardous work than girls.

ILO goes on to define four "worst forms" of labor by children, which should never be allowed. One is slavery, debt bondage, or other forms of forced labor. This includes forced recruitment of children for armed conflict, as was mentioned earlier. Other "worst forms" include involving children in illegal activities, such as producing or selling drugs; and any work that "is likely to harm the health, safety, or morals of children."

Forced labor is the type of work most similar to prison. Teens involved in forced labor have no choice in what they are doing. Often, they are not free to leave if they wish. The situation is much like prison, even if there are no actual bars.

For some jobs, the dangers are clear. Child soldiers risk being killed in conflict every day. Teens forced to carry drugs for cartels may get shot during ongoing drug wars. Others may be arrested. However, young people doing non-prohibited jobs may also face extreme health dangers. For example, gold and coal miners face dangers from cave ins and breathing dust and gasses. Children working at brick-making kilns get burns from flying ashes and breathe in harmful dust. Waste pickers often get stomach diseases; some contract life-threatening tetanus by getting cuts from rusty objects.

But even jobs that may not at first appear hazardous carry health risks for teens. Children working in agriculture may be injured by sharp tools, and some teens inhale poisonous pesticides. Teens who work in the restaurant industry frequently get burns. Those who make clothing or carpets often get cuts from the machinery and might even lose fingers.

In recent years, there have also been several catastrophes at garment factories in Asia. In November 2012, a fire raced through a garment factory in Bangladesh. More than 100 workers died.

This collapse of a garment factory in Bangladesh in 2011 killed more than 1,100 people.

Most were women, but some were teens. A similar fire two months earlier in Pakistan claimed nearly 300 lives.

An even worse incident occurred in Bangladesh in 2011. An eight-story building housing several garment companies collapsed. This tragedy killed more than 1,100 workers and injured as many as 2,500 others. Many of the victims were teens. The companies housed in the building made apparel for fifteen international retailers. A teen who was pulled to safety from the rubble that day told CBS News a year later that she had been afraid to enter the building that day because she saw cracks in the wall. A supervisor slapped her face and told her to get inside. Despite her close call with death, she planned to get another factory job. Her family needed the money.

# FAIR TRADE GOODS AND PREVENTING CHILD LABOR

Because the abuse of child laborers takes place mostly in faraway countries, it may not seem to involve us. In addition, we may feel powerless to do anything about the situation. In reality, the situation does involve us, and there are things we can do. First of all, we can check the labels of the clothes, food, and sports equipment we buy. Do they come from countries that exploit young workers? If so, we can consider alternatives made elsewhere.

Many consumers look for products that carry a Fair Trade label. That label ensures two things. First, it indicates that the items were produced in ways that protect the environment. Second, it shows that the companies that produced them provide fair wages to their workers. Fair Trade labels appear on cotton, cocoa, coffee, sugar, and more.

Child labor represents not just an economic issue; it is also a social justice issue. UNESCO's Declaration of the Rights of the Child proclaims that all children should be entitled to receive an education. They should not be allowed to work "before an appropriate minimum age." When a child works, that child should not "engage in any occupation or employment which would prejudice his health or education, or interfere with his physical, mental, or moral development." More than 190 countries throughout the world have signed this declaration. Not all live up to its standards, however.

Simply boycotting products from countries that use child labor won't help much. Real change must take place at the country level. The goal is to help countries develop economies whereby child labor is not needed to pick crops or produce materials. Meanwhile, the goal is also to help individual families reach a financial situation that allows them to prioritize sending their children to school rather than to work.

# CHAPTER FIVE

# Looking Ahead

After reading about the circumstances that affect teen prisoners (both juvenile offenders and child laborers), it might seem that the outlook is bleak. However, activists, researchers, and other concerned parties are working hard to ensure that every teen around the world has the resources and support to achieve their full potential.

## GOOD NEWS, PROMISING PRACTICES

Despite high-profile tragedies, there is some good news to report regarding child labor around the world. Overall, the number of child laborers worldwide has dropped in recent years. In 2000, it stood at 245 million, according to the International Labour Organization. By 2012, that figure had dropped to 168 million. Similarly, the number of young people involved in hazardous

*Opposite*: Providing educational opportunities is one way to break the cycle of teenage girls trapped in low-paying factory jobs.

work also dropped by more than half. That leaves roughly 85 million youngsters doing dangerous jobs. Still, it represents significant progress over the course of the past decade or so.

After the tragic building collapse in Bangladesh, some major multinational companies took steps to protect young workers. More than twenty garment and retail brands that get materials from Bangladesh signed an agreement to establish a fire and building safety program for the country. They further agreed to allow the ILO to enforce the new safety standards. Walmart, meanwhile, said that it would conduct in-depth safety inspections at all Bangladeshi factories that supply the company with goods. This type of pressure from the companies that buy their goods is likely to make factory owners pay closer attention to providing safer working conditions.

Some countries, too, are taking increased steps to protect young workers. Still, the process takes time. Sometimes it runs into unexpected roadblocks. For instance, Bolivia faced an interesting dilemma when it tried to keep the minimum working age at fourteen. In a country where approximately 20 percent of the children between the ages of seven and fourteen work, thousands of children protested. Sadly, they wanted the legal working age lowered so that they could earn money. The government gave in and lowered the legal working age to ten. The government maintains that even if it prohibited child labor, many young people would work anyway. By making child labor legal, the government says it can monitor and ensure that workers are treated fairly, removing the risk of forced labor.

## NEXT STEPS TOWARD PROTECTING CHILD LABORERS

Educating both children and employers about the dangers of various jobs is a good first step in reducing injury. At the country level, those nations that have adopted ILO Convention 138 can live up its measures. Governments can put strong protective policies in place. Then they need to follow up and enforce them.

The most effective measures, however, may come from the major multinational companies that get their products from countries that use child labor. They can pressure their contractors not to exploit child laborers. They can threaten to withhold product orders if they find their contractors breaking this agreement. Enforcing such a mandate might be difficult at first. It would require frequent, rigorous inspections. In time, however, contractors would realize that they must treat their young employees fairly. Otherwise, they risk losing their biggest customers.

According to one research study, paying a living wage to workers in Brazil, Russia, India, and China (four major sources for Western European textiles and clothing) would raise the price of goods by about 6 percent. It's uncertain whether customers would be willing to pay that much more for products if they knew the extra cost ensured that the young workers who made those products received a fair wage. We will only find out if such a plan is actually implemented.

## NEXT STEPS TOWARD ADDRESSING JUVENILE CRIME

Analyzing juvenile crime statistics trends can cause extreme pessimism—or extreme optimism. It all depends on how one interprets the data. First, the good news. Overall, juvenile crime has dropped dramatically over the past decade. According to the U.S. Department of Justice's OJJDP, law enforcement agencies made just over 1 million arrests of juveniles under the age of eighteen in 2014. At first, that may sound like a lot—and it is. However, this figure represents a 50 percent drop from the number of juvenile arrests made in 2005.

Of those million arrests in 2014, 53,500 were for violent crimes. These included murder, manslaughter, rape, robbery, and aggravated assault. That represented a drop of 44 percent from 2005. Property crimes such as burglary, arson, and motor vehicle theft also dropped by 44 percent.

These trends mirror a drop in adult crime in the United States. The overall murder rate in the United States has dropped by nearly 50 percent since the mid-1990s. Experts cite several reasons for the trend at the adult level. These include increased incarceration and longer sentences, which keeps more criminals off the streets longer. Improved law enforcement strategies are another factor. Computer analysis and innovative technology helps law enforcement officials solve more crimes. Finally, the decline of the crack cocaine epidemic also helps. This epidemic peaked in the 1980s and has dramatically declined since then.

Researchers also have identified other possible factors that may contribute to the ongoing drop in crime. Some cite the removal of lead from gasoline and paint in the 1970s. Arguing that exposure to lead causes aggressive behavior, these researchers say that lessened exposure for children born after that time may have played a role. Other researchers believe the strong economy of the 1990s and much of the 2000s may have reduced people's need to gain income through illegal means.

## A MATTER OF PERCEPTION

Despite the data, many Americans still feel unsafe. Many people perceive the nation's crime rate to be rising, even though the data show otherwise. The same holds true for juvenile crime. Some adults hold the opinion that today's teens are more violent than past generations. They believe today's teens have less sense of right and wrong. Professor James Alan Fox of Northeastern University blames the growth of crime shows and the way the media sensationalize crimes. "One case of a random, horrific shooting shown repeatedly on TV has more visceral effect than all the statistics printed in a newspaper," Fox says.

For example, news coverage of a "flash mob" of teens creating a disturbance in Philadelphia dominated headlines in that city for nearly a week in March 2017. Around the same time, the *Chicago Tribune* ran an article about how street gang thieves broke into a boxcar in a rail yard on Chicago's South Side and found boxes of brand-new guns. In North Carolina, an eighteen-year-old made headlines for allegedly beheading his mother with a knife. Those are isolated incidents. Still, headlines about real-life cases such as these often sway public opinion far more than abstract numbers about overall nationwide crime rates.

## GOING AFTER GANGS

One area where everyone agrees that challenges remain involves gangs. The estimated number of gangs in the United States has not changed much over the past twenty years. It stood at 30,800 in 1996. After dipping to a low of 20,100 in 2003, it gradually rose again. The number stood at 30,700 in 2012, almost exactly the same as it was twenty years earlier, according to the OJJDP. These gangs had a total of roughly 850,000 members. Again, this almost exactly matches the total from 1996.

Of course, not all gang members are teens. Not much demographic data exists about gangs. Data from the 1990s suggests that roughly half of all gang members are seventeen years old or younger. Another 37 percent are between the ages of eighteen and twenty-four.

When people think of gangs, they picture drug trafficking and violence. In fact, gang-related homicides in the United States totaled 2,363 in 2012. Between 2007 and 2012, gang homicides averaged nearly 2,000 per year. The 2012 figure represented a significant increase. According to FBI estimates, the United States averaged 15,500 homicides per year between 2007 and 2011. This suggests that gangs accounted for about 13 percent of total homicides (more than one out of every eight).

Chicago and Los Angeles are considered the "gang capitals" of the United States. Roughly one out of every four gang homicides recorded in the National Youth Gang Survey from 2011 to 2012 took place in one of those two cities.

According to some estimates, Chicago has more than 600 gangs or gang factions. (A faction is a subgroup of a gang.) Across the city, as many as 150,000 people (most of them juveniles) belong to gangs. Gangs regularly fight over territory for their share of the drug trade that finances many of their activities, and often these fights turn deadly. Chicago saw a record 747 murders in 2016. Some people estimate that as many as half of all homicides in Chicago are gang-related.

In 2011, Chicago police conducted a city-wide audit of gang activity. Not surprisingly, they found a heavy concentration of gangs in the city's notorious South Side. But the audit also found gangs sprinkled throughout most areas of the city. "Most of our violence is gang related, much of it is narcotics gang related," said then-Chicago Police Supt. Garry McCarthy at a press conference discussing the audit results. "They argue over turf and get into violent disputes with each other, and that's how people get hurt."

Because of statistics such as this, many people view gangs as strictly an urban problem. Statistics show otherwise. No one is totally immune from the threat of gang violence. According to the US government's National Gang Center, 41.6 percent of gangs are centered in larger cities. The rest are spread among smaller cities, suburban counties, and rural counties. Gang problems remain most persistent in major cities, however. Two out of three gang homicides occur in cities with populations over 100,000.

According to the National Gang Youth Survey, police used the following strategies most frequently to combat gang problems: 1) targeted patrols (76 percent), 2) dedicated gang unit/officer (64 percent), and 3) participation in a multiagency gang task force (52 percent). Nearly half of respondents also

Gangs account for as many as half of homicides in Chicago.

used a curfew ordinance. None of those actions will really stop gang violence. The only true solutions lie deeper.

## ADDRESSING THE ROOT PROBLEMS

Many experts believe the only way to effectively address teen crime is to address the underlying causes. These include poverty, unstable family situations, and lack of success in school. A 2015 report from the Prison Policy Initiative found that the median annual income for incarcerated people in the United States (before they were jailed) was less than half of what it was for non-incarcerated people. These statistics are for adults, but poverty certainly affects juvenile crime rates as well.

On a global basis, addressing the problems of teens held prisoner by economic and cultural situations may prove even more challenging. Some people suggest simply boycotting products that may be made by child laborers. That approach may create as many problems as it solves. The economies of many developing countries depend on the type of inexpensive labor that young workers provide. Furthermore, many struggling

Strengthening educational systems helps create new opportunities for young people, such as for these children in Zimbabwe.

families depend on the small incomes that children generate. Even the teens themselves might not want to be "rescued" from their working situation. Bad as it may be, for many children, it's the only alternative.

Ideally, improving the situation for these teens involves helping the countries developing a more stable economy that does not require their labor. It also involves helping countries see the value of education for all its young people, including girls. However, such systemic change can take years. In countries wracked by civil war or other internal struggles, the challenge becomes even greater.

## WHY DOES IT MATTER?

Reducing juvenile delinquency and the number of incarcerated teens should be a priority for many reasons. Society should want as few people as possible in prison or forced labor situations. In the case of teens in detention centers, it's an economic issue, too. According to a CBS News report in 2014, America spends $80 billion each year on incarceration. That comes to more than $250 for every US resident.

The exact figures for juvenile incarceration costs are not quite as recent. However, according to the American Correctional Association, the average daily cost nationwide to incarcerate one juvenile offender in 2008 was $241. That translates to $88,000 per year per youth. Given the number of juveniles incarcerated in 2008, that made the total cost of juvenile incarceration $5.7 billion. The average daily cost of incarceration has no doubt risen since then.

Meanwhile, the average annual cost of educating a student in public school in the United States totaled $12,296 for the 2012–2013 school year. That means it costs at least seven times as much for a teen to be in a detention facility as opposed to being in school.

Clearly, reducing crime rates and the numbers of people incarcerated saves money. With that in mind, it makes sense to invest in rehabilitation programs for juveniles. By helping troubled teens get back on the right road, society may help prevent them from committing more serious crimes in the future. This benefits both them and society.

Economists also urge considering the costs of lost potential and productivity. Teens who are in detention facilities are not working. They are not furthering their education and are less likely to graduate high school. They are not preparing themselves for a productive future. (This is also true of teens who must work instead of attending school.)

## EFFECTIVE JUVENILE DELINQUENCY INTERVENTION PROGRAMS

Over the years, authorities have tried many different types of intervention programs to help juvenile delinquents. The goal is to reduce recidivism rates and help juveniles find a better path forward.

Some programs focus on prevention; others focus on working with teens who have already been in trouble. The US government's National Institute of Justice (NIJ) maintains a database of such programs and rates their effectiveness. NIJ rated 237 programs focusing on delinquency prevention. It found 22 percent of them effective, 57 percent considered promising, and 21 percent as having no effects.

In the 1990s, researcher M. W. Lipsey found that more effective intervention programs had several common elements. These programs provided more and longer treatment, they were designed by a researcher or had a research component, and they offered behavioral, skill-oriented, and multimodal treatment. There was also evidence that treatment provided in detention facilities was less effective than in other settings

Researchers at the University of Maryland reached similar conclusions in 1997. For instance, they concluded that many solutions to juvenile crime and delinquency are best found outside of the criminal justice system. They also noted that high-crime areas that most needed innovative programs were the most difficult to reach. In addition, they asserted that social conditions, such as social inequality and concentrated poverty, contribute heavily to crime and delinquency.

The Maryland researchers concluded that Department of Justice resources should be directed "to the urban neighborhoods where youth violence is highly concentrated." They noted that homicide rates in these areas of concentrated poverty are twenty times the national average.

## A NEW MODEL: RESTORATIVE JUSTICE

In the past, the justice system in the United States tended to focus on either retribution or rehabilitation. Retribution emphasized punishment. The idea was that if the punishment was harsh enough, it would discourage people from breaking the law. Hallmarks of this system are long sentences and less use of probation and parole.

Rehabilitation, on the other hand, focuses on helping criminals learn how to change their behavior. Under this model, the justice system provides education and job skills. If criminals struggled with drug addiction or psychological problems, the system provides counseling to help them overcome those challenges. Of course, these services cost money. Therefore, this approach is more expensive in the short term. The goal is to help prisoners serve shorter sentences and equip them with skills that will reduce the rate of recidivism. That would save the system money over the long-term because of the high ongoing cost of keeping prisoners behind bars.

Restorative justice takes an entirely different approach. The idea is to bring criminals together with their victims. This way, criminals understand the effect of their actions. The hope is that this will deter them from doing similar things in the future. At first glance, this approach may seem unrealistic. Does it create real remorse in the offender? Will it change his or her future behavior? Do the victims or their families even want to meet the people who wronged them? Restorative justice is hardly a new concept. It has been used in some cultures for thousands of years. Today, it serves as the primary model of juvenile justice in New Zealand. In North America, the model first emerged in Canada in the 1970s and gradually spread to the United States. It doesn't work in every case, but overall it shows great promise.

The idea of restorative justice makes special sense in dealing with juvenile offenders. Many young people have been arrested for non-serious crimes. Even if their crimes are more serious, it may be their first offense. Restorative justice encourages young people to turn around their lives around before they become hardened criminals. This has several potential benefits. It may help the young people become productive citizens. It may lower the long-term costs of incarceration if it prevents the juveniles from being repeat offenders. Finally, it may help bring healing to the victims and their families.

The state of Colorado passed a restorative justice bill in 2013. The bill focused on juvenile offenders and built on programs that had been previously established around the state. For instance, the town of Longmont runs two restorative justice programs. One operates in the community, and the other focuses on local schools. In the school program, which is voluntary, the offender and victim talk about the incident and its impact in front of others. At the end of the process, the offender signs a contract to do community service instead of serving jail time. In some years, more than 1,000 people participate in the program.

Virginia Purata wishes she had been offered the program when she was suspended as a freshman in high school. When she heard about the program two years later, she became a volunteer. She went on to become an assistant coordinator for the program. "The thing that caught my attention was that it was giving people second chances," Purata told a local newspaper. "I know a little bit about making a mistake and wishing you could take it back, and I thought that was something worth being involved in."

Nationwide, the recidivism rate among adult criminals typically runs between 60 and 70 percent. In Longmont, the recidivism rate among participants in the juvenile program stands at 10 percent. Proponents also point out that it saves thousands of dollars per case by keeping youth out of detention centers.

Restorative justice is not the only answer to juvenile crime, but it may be one of the answers. It's one way to help avoid the "school to prison pipeline" in which troubled teens find

Restorative Justice programs such as this one in Longmont, Colorado, may help reduce recidivism rates.

themselves drawn into a life of crime from which they cannot easily escape.

## RETHINKING JUVENILE JUSTICE

Some reformers believe that simply changing programs won't change things. They argue that we should reconsider the entire juvenile justice system. In a book called *Reforming Juvenile Justice*, the National Research Council of the National Academies of Sciences recommends some research-based changes that might be made.

The National Research Council describes a "Positive Youth Justice" model. The model focuses on youths' strengths rather than their deficits. The concept started for use with youth in general. However, researchers believe the model can also work well with juvenile offenders.

The Juvenile Justice and Delinquency Prevention Act calls for states to support programs for positive youth development. Specifically, it calls for helping at-risk youth obtain five key things: 1) a sense of safety and structure, 2) a sense of belonging and membership, 3) a sense of self-worth and social contribution, 4) a sense of independence and control over one's life, and 5) a sense of closeness in interpersonal relationships.

The report gives examples of the concept in action. In Florida, teenage girls in a semi-secure juvenile residential facility planned and implemented a special service project. The teens helped grandparents who were raising their grandchildren in high-crime neighborhoods in their town. They helped the seniors with shopping and other chores, and they even created oral histories for the seniors. Meanwhile, in Pennsylvania, juvenile offenders worked with adults to plan and maintain a community garden. Their day treatment program served as an alternative to incarceration. Both programs got youth and adults to work together in positive ways to support the community.

The report authors conclude by comparing the Positive Youth Justice program to the food pyramid. "Just as a balanced diet needs to contain more than starches and meat, an effective approach to youth justice should include more than job training or anger management, more than just drug treatment or community service. The best youth development strategies include a diverse menu of services, opportunities, and support."

## HOPE FOR THE FUTURE

Clearly, finding effective ways of keeping teens in school and out of trouble serves everyone's best interests. The best solution would be find ways to address the root causes that lead to both crime and forced labor arrangements while children are young. Providing education, health care, and social services helps more children lead more stable lives. Targeting programs to high-poverty areas where gangs thrive can also help deter teens from committing crimes.

Despite all best efforts, some teens will continue to break the law. In those cases, the juvenile justice system must provide treatment that both protects society and rehabilitates offenders. According to CBS News, more than two out of three adult offenders (68 percent) were arrested for a new crime within three years after being released from prison. More than three out of four (77 percent) were re-arrested within five years.

Earning a high school diploma is a key step toward leading a productive life.

Similar statistics are not available for juveniles, as there is no national data available. Each state measures recidivism in different ways. In any case, it is clear that reducing recidivism must be a primary goal for all juvenile justice programs. This serves the best interests both for the offenders and for society at large.

In many ways, the juvenile justice system represents a crossroads for teen offenders. If they take one path, they can turn their life around. They can complete their education and become productive members of society. Completing school is also the hope for child laborers. Often the circumstances at home that lead teens in the United States (and around the world) to break the law are similar to the circumstances that land teens in exploitative working conditions. Addressing the issues teens face is our best hope for protecting them, no matter where they live. In the cases of teen offenders and teen laborers, the implications—both for them and for society at large—are enormous.

# TURNING IT AROUND

Stories about teens committing crimes tend to grab the headlines. But occasionally teens who successfully turn things around make the news as well. Lt. Craig Martinez serves as the public information officer for the Orem (UT) police force. Prior to this position, he worked as a detective, S.W.A.T. member, patrol officer, US air marshal, high patrol officer, and US Marine. But it wasn't always that way. As a teen, Martinez shoplifted and burglarized cars. Then he became a teen father. Having a child convinced him to turn his life around, and he joined the Marines, which gave his life discipline. After four years in the Marines, he became a law enforcement officer. Now on the other side of the handcuffs, he uses his past experiences to relate to troubled teens. By sharing his story, he hopes to convince other teens to avoid the mistakes he made.

A number of celebrities also overcame rough teen years to achieve fame. Rapper Snoop Dogg was convicted of drug possession. Former heavyweight boxing champion Mike Tyson was arrested multiple times by the age of thirteen. One of his juvenile detention center counselors introduced him to boxing trainer Cus D'Amato, who became his mentor. NBA Hall of Famer Allen Iverson served time in prison as a teen

NBA Hall of Famer Allen Iverson overcame troubled teen years to become a basketball superstar.

for his role in a bowling alley brawl. All of these stories show that troubled teens can turn their lives around.

**"affluenza"** A term created to describe a condition in which wealthy youth feel guilt, lack of motivation, and social isolation.

**bonded labor** Work done to repay a debt or other obligation.

**bootstrapping** Adding more charges to a single criminal incident.

**complexion** The way something looks or is made up.

**contempt of court** Disregarding a court order or not showing proper respect in court.

**criminogenic** A situation relating to crime or likely to cause criminal behavior.

**curfew** A regulation that requires people to remain inside between certain hours; curfews often are used specifically for young people.

**deinstitutionalization** Placing people outside of formal institutions for detention or treatment.

**delinquency** A minor crime, especially relating to young people.

**disparity** A large difference.

**disproportionate** Too much or too many when compared to something else or compared to what is expected.

**diversion** The process of moving something or someone from one course to another.

**entrenched** Firmly established, such as a habit or belief.

**epidemic** A widespread or out of control problem.

**exploitation** A situation that takes advantage of a person.

**homicide** Murder.

**incarceration** The state of being confined, as in prison.

**jurisdiction** The area of legal authority for a court or other justice system.

**juvenile**  Relating to young people.

**larceny**  Theft or stealing.

**living wage**  A wage that provides workers with a reasonable standard of living.

**mandatory**  Required; offering no choice.

**mediate**  To work to help people resolve a dispute.

**parole**  The release of a prisoner before the completion of his or her sentence, generally for good behavior.

**probation**  The release of an offender under certain terms of supervision.

**Progressive movement**  A movement toward social reform marked by new or liberal ideas.

**recidivism**  The tendency of a criminal to commit more offenses in the future.

**reform schools**  Institutions where juvenile offenders are sent to learn how to change their behavior.

**rehabilitation**  Helping someone return to normal life after imprisonment or addiction through therapy or treatment.

**restorative justice** A system that focuses on bringing criminals together with victims to promote understanding and healing.

**retribution** Punishment for a criminal act.

**social reformers** People who work to change the way society operates.

**status offenders** People whose offense is determined by their status, in this case age.

**Sumangali system** A form of child labor in India where young women are supposedly earning money toward getting married.

**truancy** Being absent from school without an excused reason.

# FURTHER INFORMATION

## Books

Bernstein, Neil. *Burning Down the House: The End of Juvenile Prison.* New York: The New Press, 2016.

Humes, Edward. *No Matter How Loud I Shout: A Year in the Life of Juvenile Justice.* New York: Simon & Schuster, 2015.

Myers, Walter Dean. *Lockdown.* New York: Amistad, 2011.

Shoemaker, Donald J. and Timothy W. Wolfe. *Juvenile Justice.* 2nd ed. Santa Barbara, CA: ABC-CLIO, 2016.

## Websites

### Behind Bars: Four Teens in Prison Tell Their Stories
http://www.layouth.com/behind-bars-four-teens-in-prison
-tell-their-stories/
L. A. Youth offers compelling true stories from actual teens about their experiences in the juvenile justice system.

## Child Labor

http://www.ilo.org/global/topics/child-labour/lang--en/index.htm

The website of the International Labour Organization provides statistics, news, and resources relating to child labor worldwide.

## A Day in the Life of Detention

http://www.clallam.net/JuvenileServices/dayindetention.html

The Juvenile and Family Services website of Clallam County, Washington, gives details about life in the juvenile detention center.

## Juvenile Justice

http://youth.gov/youth-topics/juvenile-justice

Explore information about the juvenile justice process, risk factors, new prevention ideas, and more.

## Office of Juvenile Justice and Delinquency Prevention

https://www.ojjdp.gov/index.html

Learn more about the US Government's Office of Juvenile Justice and Delinquency Prevention, including their latest programs.

## Videos

### "College Program Inspires Young Inmates"

http://www.nbcnews.com/video/nightly-news/47346039

NBC News showcases a program for juvenile offenders in adult prisons that provides educational opportunities and combats recidivism.

### "Inmates in Georgia Give Teens a Taste of Prison Life"

http://www.aetv.com/shows/beyond-scared-straight/seas on-3/episode-13/inmates-in-georgia-give-teens-a-taste-of -prison-life

This segment from A&E's *Beyond Scared Straight* series takes some Georgia juveniles behind bars to see everyday life in prison.

Abbey, Jennifer, Candace Smith, and Matt Rosenbaum. "Chicago Gang Life: Gang Members Talk About Life on the Streets, Heartache." ABC News, October 19, 2012. http://abcnews.go.com/US/chicago-gang-life-gang-members-talks-life-streets/story?id=17499354#2.

Bryen, Whitney. "Longmont Program Highlights Restorative Justice Potential." *Longmont Times-Call*, July 13, 2013. http://www.timescall.com/news/longmont-local-news/ci_23656592/longmont-program-highlights-restorative-justice-potential.

Burke, Jason and Saad Hammadi. "Bangladesh Textile Factory Fire Leaves More Than 100 Dead." *The Guardian*, November 25, 2012. https://www.theguardian.com/world/2012/nov/25/bangladesh-textile-factory-fire.

Butts, Jeffrey A., Gordon Bazemore, and Aundra Saa Meroe. *Positive Youth Justice: Framing Justice Interventions Using the Concepts of Positive Youth Development.* Washington, DC: Coalition for Juvenile Justice, 2010.

Cauffman, Elizabeth, Frances J. Lexcen, Asha Goldweb, Elizabeth P. Shulman, and Thomas Grisso. "Gender Differences in Mental Health Symptoms Among Delinquent and Community Youth." Youth Violence and Juvenile Justice, July 1, 2007. http://journals.sagepub.com/doi/abs/10.1177/1541204007301292.

Dugan, Emily. "Most Young Men in Gangs 'Suffer Psychiatric Illness.'" *Independent*, July 11, 2013. http://www.independent.co.uk/news/uk/home-news/most-young-men-in-gangs-suffer-psychiatric-illness-8703986.html.

Egley, Jr., Arlen, James C. Howell, and Meena Harris. "Highlights of the 2012 National Youth Gang Survey." OJJDP, December 2014. https://www.ojjdp.gov/pubs/248025.pdf.

Finley, Laura L. *Juvenile Justice*. Westport, CT: Greenwood, 2007.

Flores, Jerry. *Caught Up: Girls, Surveillance, and Wraparound Incarceration*. Oakland, CA: University of California Press, 2016.

Fries, Laura. "Review: Scared Straight." *Variety*, April 14, 1999. http://variety.com/1999/film/reviews/scared-straight-20-years-later-1200457295/.

Goldstein, Barry, and John Muncie, eds. *Youth Crime & Justice*. 2nd ed. Thousand Oaks, CA: Sage Publications, 2015.

Haberman, Clyde. "When Youth Violence Spurred 'Super-Predator' Fear." *New York Times*, April 6, 2014. https://www.nytimes.com/2014/04/07/us/politics/killing-on-bus-recalls-superpredator-threat-of-90s.html?_r=0.

Hamilton, Brad. "Rise of the Girl Gangs," *New York Post*, December 4, 2011. http://nypost.com/2011/12/04/rise-of-the-girl-gangs/.

Hudson, Don. "How a Law-Breaking Teen Became a Law Enforcement Officer." Good4Utah.com, March 3, 2017. http://www.good4utah.com/news/local-news/from-criminal-to-cop-how-a-problem-child-became-a-policeman/666411617.

Kanazawa, Satoshi. "Why Are Almost All Criminals men?" *Psychology Today*, July 3, 2008. https://www.psychologytoday.com/blog/the-scientific-fundamentalist/200807/why-are-almost-all-criminals-men-part-i.

Kennedy, Bruce. "The Bangladesh Factory Collapse One Year Later." CBS News, April 23, 2014. http://www.cbsnews.com/news/the-bangladesh-factory-collapse-one-year-later/.

L. A. Youth. "Behind Bars: Four Teens in Prison Tell Their Stories." Retrieved April 1, 2017. http://www.layouth. com/behind-bars-four-teens-in-prison-tell-their-stories/.

McNamara, Brittney. "Some States Are Still Sending Teens to Adult Prisons." *Teen Vogue*, March 20, 2017. http:// www.teenvogue.com/story/some-states-still-send-teens-to-adult-prison.

Mendel, Richard A. *No Place for Kids: The Case for Reducing Juvenile Incarceration*. Baltimore, Maryland: Annie E. Casey Foundation, 2011. http://www.aecf.org/m/resourcedoc/aecf-NoPlaceForKidsFullReport-2011.pdf.

Picchi, Aimee. "The High Price of Incarceration in America." CBS News, May 8, 2014. http://www.cbsnews. com/news/the-high-price-of-americas-incarceration-80-billion/.

PRIME Education. "Case Management Within the Walls of Teen Residential Programs." August 1, 2009. https:// primeinc.org/casestudies/casemanager/study/123/Case_ Management_Within_the_Walls_of_Teen_Residential_ Programs.

Rabuy, Bernadette, and Daniel Kopf. "Prisons of Poverty: Uncovering the Pre-incarceration Incomes of the Imprisoned." Prison Policy Initiative, July 9, 2015. https://www.prisonpolicy.org/reports/income.html.

Ramos, Elliot. "In Chicago, Gangs Abound, but Where Are They?" WBEZ91.5, February 29, 2016. https://www.wbez.org/shows/wbez-news/in-chicago-gangs-abound-but-where-are-they/0d956c2e-171a-483a-8666-f5228d98812d.

Rovner, Josh. "Juvenile Life Without Parole: An Overview." The Sentencing Project, March 22, 2017. http://www.sentencingproject.org/publications/juvenile-life-without-parole/.

Salvatore, Christopher. *Arrested Adolescent Offenders*. El Paso, TX: LBF Scholarly Publishing, LLC, 2013.

Shoemaker, Donald J., and Timothy W. Wolfe. *Juvenile Justice*. 2d ed. Santa Barbara, CA: ABC-CLIO, 2016.

Soyer, Michaela. *A Dream Denied: Incarceration, Recidivism, and Young Minority Men in America*. Oakland, CA: University of California Press, 2016.

Tapia, Mike. *Juvenile Arrest in America: Race, Social Class, and Gang Membership*. El Paso, TX: LBF Scholarship Publishing, LLC, 2010.

Watson, Liz, and Peter Edelman. *Improving the Juvenile Justice System for Girls: Lessons from the States*. Washington, DC: Georgetown Center on Poverty, Inequality and Public Policy, 2012. http://www.law.georgetown.edu/academics/

centers-institutes/poverty-inequality/upload/JDS_V1R4_
Web_Singles.pdf.

Wood, Daniel B. "US Crime Rate at Lowest Point in
Decades. Why America Is Safer Now." *Christian Science
Monitor*, January 9, 2012. http://www.csmonitor.com/
USA/Justice/2012/0109/US-crime-rate-at-lowest-point-
in-decades.-Why-America-is-safer-now.

Page numbers in **boldface** are illustrations. Entries in **boldface** are glossary terms.

# ABOUT THE AUTHOR

**John Micklos Jr.** is an award-winning education journalist and the author of more than thirty books for children and young adult readers. His works include poetry books for young readers, history books for elementary students, and history and biography titles for middle school and high school students. He also contributed to National Geographic Kids' popular book *125 True Stories of Amazing Pets*. His newest books include *The Sound in the Basement* and *Beach Fun: Poems of Surf and Sand*, picture books published by First State Press, along with *One Leaf, Two Leaves, Count with Me*, published by Penguin. Learn more at John's website, www. JohnMicklosWriter.com.